Beginner's Guide to Investing

Successful Investing 1?

Entrepreneur Series

Manuel Taylor

Mendon Cottage Books

JD-Biz Publishing

Disclaimer

The information is this book is provided for informational purposes only. It is not intended to be used and medical advice or a substitute for proper medical treatment by a qualified health care provider. The information is believed to be accurate as presented based on research by the author.

The contents have not been evaluated by the U.S. Food and Drug Administration or any other Government or Health Organization and the contents in this book are not to be used to treat cure or prevent disease.

The author or publisher is not responsible for the use or safety of any diet, procedure, or treatment mentioned in this book. The author or publisher is not responsible for errors or omissions that may exist.

Warning

The Book is for informational purposes only and before taking on any diet, treatment, or medical procedure, it is recommended to consult with your primary health care provider.

Our books are available at
1. Amazon.com
2. Barnes and Noble
3. Itunes
4. Kobo
5. Smashwords
6. Google Play Books

Table of Contents

Introduction – Why people invest?

Investing simply means putting your money to work for you. The reason why people invest is pretty obvious – **to get rich(er).**

Arnold Schwarzenegger once said that money does not make people happy. According to what he said, he has over $50 million, but he is just as happy as he was when he had $48 million. Now that is easy to say when you have that much money right?

Most of the people that think that the rich are lucky. But that's wrong. Most of the rich people actually earned their money. They found what they are good at, they used their skills and qualities and earned the money. Being rich does not mean that you are lucky. It means that you have found out how to use what you are good at to make money.

However, there is something that almost all rich and smart people know. They know the power of compounding interest. They know the power of investing and putting your money to work for you. They know the power of the compounding interest. If you don't know what it means, don't worry, in the next couple of pages you will understand everything there is about it.

Here's what the famous Albert Einstein said about it:

"Compounded interest is the 8th wonder of the world. He who understands it, earns it. He who doesn't, pays it."

Why is this so important? Well, let's take a look at a short example.

If you have $10.000 and you are able to invest them somewhere and get a return of 10% per year, would you use this opportunity or will you pass it? Most people will pass on this because they don't like to give up the money they have, regardless of what they get as reward. Most people will pass on this because of the thought they actually have to give up $10.000. But, let's take a look at what happens if you actually invest and do that for more than one year.

If you invest the $10.000, at the end of year one, you get $11.000, that's the original investment of $10.000 plus interest of $1.000.

If you reinvest this amount, you are going to get $12.100 at the end of year 2. Your interest is not $1.000 as it was in the previous year, it is $1.100 now! You get interest on the interest you earned during year one. That's what compounding interest is, interest on interest.

Now, you may still wonder why this is important. Let's take a look at what happens after 10, 20, 30, 40 and 50 years.

Year 1	$	11,000
Year 2	$	12,100
Year 10	$	25,937
Year 20	$	67,275
Year 30	$	174,494
Year 40	$	452,593
Year 50	$	1,173,909

Wait, is that a million? By investing only $10.000? YES! IT IS A MILLION! Well, imagine what would happen if you invested more money, or if you invested at higher return rate! No wonder Einstein was fascinated by the power of compounding interest. By investing only $10.000 at interest rate of 10%, you become millionaire after 50 years! Smart people invest because they know what this means.

Most people think they cannot afford to invest, because they have debt and credit cards and bills to pay. Well, I disagree. I think that any person can afford to take $200 from the monthly salary, invest the money and then forget about them for couple of years. You choose the side, will you earn the compound interest or will you pay it? Make sure you make the right decision.

Chapter 1 – The relation between Risk and Return

Robert Arnott, an American Entrepreneur once said "In investing, what is comfortable is rarely profitable."

The Chinese symbol for risk is a combination of two signs. The first sign represents danger or crisis and the second one represents opportunity. This represents both sides of the risk, the downside and the upside. The relation between risk and return is positively correlated. If you are willing to take a higher risk, you want a higher return as a reward. This reward is called risk premium. On the other side, if you invest in something secure such as Treasury bill or certificate of deposit, you will get lower return rate because you are almost certain that you will get the payment at the end and you are not really taking any risk. The return rate is formed the same way as everything else on the market, by the powers of supply and demand.

We are going to explain what this means through an example. Imagine that you can invest in two different businesses. There are two people that want to start businesses. The first one has 100% chance of succeeding, the second one has 50%. Which one will you choose? It's obvious, right? But, there are a lot of people that can invest in both of these businesses, it is not only you. People investing in the 100% safe business are willing to accept a low return rate and these people will fight for this business. They are going to offer rate even as low as 1%. These type of investors are risk averse. They prefer investing in what's safe.

On the other hand, there are people who are neutral towards risk or even risk lovers. The second type of investors will probably invest in the more risky business. But of course, they will demand a much higher return rate in order to compensate the risk they are taking. If the return rate was same on both, they'd obviously choose to invest in the 100% safe business.

Now, as we mentioned above, the return rate is created by two forces, the demand and the supply. The higher the demand is, the higher the return rate. The higher the supply is, the lower the return rate. The relation between the Risk and Return is positively correlated. The higher the risk, the higher the return.

If the owner of the first business that had 100% chance of succeeding asked for a loan and said that he is willing to pay 5% interest, a lot of investors will show up. However, the business owner will choose the investor that will offer the lowest interest rate. This is how the return rate is formed. In this case, the interest rate that the owner of the business pays is the return rate for the investor.

How do we measure risk?

There are two main categories of risk, financial and non-financial. Each of these categories has a lot of different risks.

Financial risks:

- *Liquidity risk* represents the possibility that the company won't be able to sell the certain good at given time, or the company will be able to sell the good at given time, but at a lower price.
- *Credit risk* – represents the possibility that the clients won't pay their obligations on time.
- *Market risk* – is a combination of risks related to the market prices of the goods.

- *Interest rate risk* – represents the possibility of movement of the market interest rate in a way that will have negative influence on the company.

Non-financial risks:

- *Tax risk* represents the possibility of a change of tax regulation in a way that will have negative influence on the company.
- *Accounting risk* represents the possibility of fraud or mistake in the accounting department.
- *Legal risk* represents the possibility of change in law that will result with a negative influence on the company.
- *Operational risk* represents the possibility of mistakes done by employees or natural disasters.

These are only some of the many risks that the businesses face. It is quite hard to quantify all of these, right? Some of the investors analyze each of these risk individually and create an opinion about the company as a whole. However, all of these risks represent the possibility of a certain event happening in the future and the future is uncertain.

On the other side, there are people that don't do all these stuff, but they use something else as a measure of risk. In finance, risk is measured using standard deviation. The standard deviation is a measure that shows the variation/dispersion. The bigger the variation/dispersion, the higher the stock is. This can be used to find out the risk level of a stock, but cannot be used to understand the risk level of a business that is not listed on a stock exchange.

The third type of investors actually do relative valuation. We'll go through this using a simple example.

Let's imagine that there is a store that you are interested in buying, however you do not know how much it is worth. You do not know the level of risk it has so you cannot make an offer without knowing that. What you can do is find a similar company on the stock market and take a look at how other investors are valuing it. You can make adjustments if you think that it is more or less risky or if it earns more or less money. This way you do not find out about the level of risk, but you discover how other people look at the same type of company.

Relative valuation is used in such cases by a lot of investors.

Chapter 2 – Most common types of investment

Today, in 21st century you can invest in almost anything. In this chapter, you are going to learn about the two different types of investing and the most common types of investment.

Here is a short list of what you can invest in:

- Certificate of deposit – This works like a saving account. You deposit money and earn interest rate on regular basis. What makes a CD (certificate of deposit) different than the saving account is that you "lock" your money for that period of time. You are not allowed to take out your money. However, you get a higher interest rate than usual because of that.

- Bonds – They are usually issued by large companies when they need money. They have higher interest rate than the Treasury bills and the certificates of deposit and they can last as little as couple of days up to several years, depending on the strategy of the corporation that is issuing the bonds.

- Mutual funds – This type of investment represents putting the money of many investors into one account and creating a portfolio of investments. There is usually a person or a team of people responsible for investing the sum of money. If you are not familiar with creating a portfolio, we will speak about it and we will create one later in this book.

- Stocks/shares – They represent part of a company. If a company has 100 shares and you own 10 shares, then you own 10% of the company. There are two types of shares. The types of shares that are pieces of the company are called common shares and they have certain advantages over the other type of shares, preferred shares. Each common share gives the owner of the share a right to vote. The preferred shares on the other hand do not give the owner a right to vote, however they are getting the dividend before the common stock owners.

- Commodities – Commodity is a raw material or an agricultural material such as gold, silver, oil, copper, beef, natural gas, lumber, sugar, coffee, rice, wheat and so on. There are people that buy commodities online and they own certain amount of them. They do not have them in a room where they live, but they virtually own them and are able to sell them at any time. People buy commodities hoping that the price of what they bought will go up and they will earn money on the difference between the buy and sell price.

- Indices – The most popular indices are the S&P 500 and the DJIA. S&P 500 stands for Standard and Poor's 500 and it includes pieces of 500 different stocks. DJI stands for Dow Jones Industrial Average.

- Forex – This type of investing is becoming a lot popular as there are a lot of people who want to become rich overnight. It involves trading of currencies and is not recommended for beginners.

The two different types of investing are **passive** and **active.** These mostly depend on your knowledge about investment and the time you can afford to spend searching for good investment options.

We've already covered the basic ones and these are enough to know for a beginner investor. The certificate of deposit and the bond as investment usually have low risk and low rate of return. There is not much to talk about these two types of investment as investing in them is simple. The real deal is investing in stocks, commodities and especially using futures.

What are futures?

Futures are contracts created by the seller and buyer to sell/buy a certain quantity of certain good at some time in the future. Why futures exist? Let's go through an example.

Let's imagine that there's a person who is selling tomatoes. In about 2 months, he will have about 300 kilograms of tomatoes available to sell. The price right now is $1.1 per kilogram. According to what happened in the past few years, the tomatoes price should drop down to $0.9 per kilogram. What this man can do is sign a future contract with a local company to sell the tomatoes for 1$ per kilogram on a specific date. Once the contract is made, he will have an obligation to sell the 300 kilograms for a price of $1 per kilogram on the specific date.

You might be asking why the local company would sign such contract if the price of tomatoes is expected to go down to $0.9. The future is uncertain. The priced went down to $0.9 the past 5 years, but it does not mean it will go down again. The price is formed by the power of supply and demand. If the supply falls due to the bad weather, not everyone on the side of the demand will be able to buy tomatoes as there won't be enough. This will increase the price of the tomatoes as some people will be willing to pay more in order to receive that particular good. On the other hand, if the demand for tomatoes increases due to openings of other similar companies, the same thing happens.

So if any of these scenarios happened, it is very likely that the price of the tomatoes may not go down to $0.9. However, the company cannot predict the weather nor the openings of other businesses in the future.

The main reason why futures exists are to reduce the risk. As you can see in this example, both the farmer and the company have reduced the risk.

However, these futures are contracts and can be sold. The farmer could sell the contract to another farmer and the company can do that same. However, the owner of the future at the particular time has to fulfil its obligation, either sell or buy the particular good. This is not a typical investment, but futures are used for making money today.

Chapter 3 – Diversification is for idiots, or not?

The rest of the book will be about investing in stocks as it is recommended for beginners.

There are a lot of people that invest money hoping to make a good return on investment. One thing that investors fight about is diversification. On the one side, there are people that say "Do not put all of your eggs in the same basket." This means you should invest in many different stocks, because you never know what the future brings.

But on the other side, there are investors that say "diversification is for idiots". They say that you should only invest in something you know. If you are diversifying, it means you are afraid that you might lose and you are afraid of that only when you don't know what you are doing.

But there is something interesting about this "fight". Even those investors who claim that diversification is for idiots have quite large portfolio of stocks. Warren Buffet, the most famous investor of all time has a portfolio of stocks of over 40 different companies. That looks pretty diversified to me.

Chapter 4 – Value investing

Value investing is what Benjamin Graham taught Warren Buffett. These type of investing basically tells investors to value the company using your own methods and find out if the price of the stock is overpriced or underpriced. If it is underpriced, it means it is a good time to buy it. However, there is a huge problem. The value you give to a company is what you think that the company is worth. Your opinion is not really important in this business.

I am going to share something that Aswath Damodaran, a professor at NYU said about value investing.

"You can be right in your assessment of value and go bankrupt being right. Your friend can pick stocks based on astrological signs and make millions. Don't expect justice."

A good example of this are the forecasts made by expert analysts. You can use google, yahoo, bing or any online search engine to find forecast for any stock.

Example, write "Microsoft forecast" and check the money.cnn.com link. On the left side, you can see the number of analysts that made a 12-month price forecast and you can see how different their opinions are about the stock price. Remember, all of these people have experience and are experts at what they do. Yet, they have very different opinions.

Stock Price Forecast

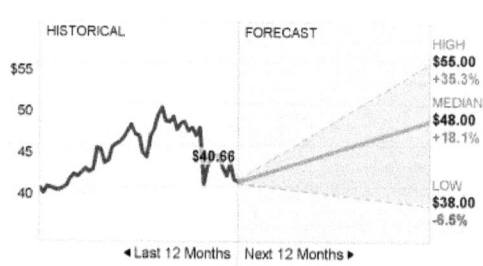

The 33 analysts offering 12-month price forecasts for Microsoft have a median target of 48.00, with a high estimate of 55.00 and a low estimate of 38.00. The median estimate represents a +18.17% increase from the last price of 40.62.

A bit under, you can see recommendations given by analysts. There are 5 different recommendations that they can choose to give: buy, outperform, hold, underperform or sell. Again, you can see that there are different opinions.

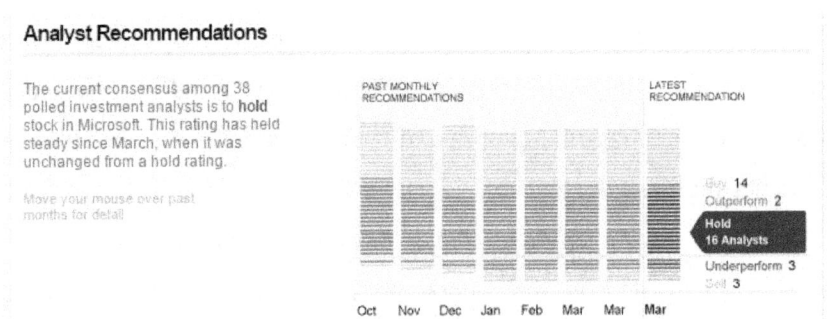

While some analysts recommend that it is a great time to buy this stock, other recommend you to stay away from it. It is a bit confusing isn't it? Aren't they supposed to agree on this? Obviously not. It does not matter who's right about the value of the company. It is important how other investors will reach on the price.

We are not going to talk a lot about value investing right now as there are a lot of different analysis that are related to that and this book is not about that.

Why is active investing riskier than passive investing?

There are small details that have huge influence on the price of the stocks.

Example:

- The stock price of the English club, Manchester united, was $15.53 on Friday. Two days later, they won 2:1 against Liverpool. The stock price was increasing during the next week and the price the next Friday was $16.45! That's increase of almost 6% for only a week.

- Tesla's price fell over 10% for a week after they announced they are cutting jobs in China.

These small details had huge impact on the prices. If you wanted to make money on short-run, and you chose Tesla, you would've lost money. However, on the long-run, the price of the stock would move up. It is hard to predict these events and this is why people recommend diversification which means buying different stocks. This allows you to compensate the losses with wins. This is what modern portfolio theory is about. This is very important when it comes to investing and that is what the next chapter is about.

Chapter 5 – Theory of portfolio optimization

One of the biggest discoveries when it comes to investing was the portfolio optimization theory. The modern portfolio theory was found by Harry Markowitz in the 1950s and it is based on some assumptions:

- Investors want maximum return for a given amount of risk that they're taking
- Correlation between assets are fixed and constant forever.
- All investors aim to maximize economic utility.
- All investors are rational.
- All investors are risk-averse.
- All investors have access to the same information at the same time.
- There are no taxes and transaction costs.

- All investors are price takers.
- Any investor can lend/borrow an unlimited amount at the risk free rate of interest.

This is where the modern portfolio theory gets criticized. However, it is working good, so far.

Another thing that Aswath Damodaran has said is "I'd rather use a model that has unrealistic assumptions, but give me good result, rather than a model with realistic assumptions that gives me false results."

The modern portfolio theory allows you to maximize the expected return on given amount of risk or minimize the risk at given expected rate of return.

In this chapter, we are going to go step by step and optimize a portfolio of 2 stocks using Excel.

The photo under is taken from Wikipedia and it contains all the information you need to know about the portfolio optimization formula. However, if you are not familiar with it or you don't know what it means, you don't have to worry. We are going to go step by step and optimize a portfolio of Microsoft and Coca-Cola.

This is all you need to know, however if you are not good at math, it is okay. We are going step by step and you will do okay.

- Portfolio return is the proportion-weighted combination of the constituent assets' returns.
- Portfolio volatility is a function of the correlations ρ_{ij} of the component assets, for all asset pairs (i, j).

In general:

- Expected return:

$$E(R_p) = \sum_i w_i E(R_i)$$

where R_p is the return on the portfolio, R_i is the return on asset i and w_i is the weighting of component asset i (that is, the proportion of asset "i" in the portfolio).

- Portfolio return variance:

$$\sigma_p^2 = \sum_i w_i^2 \sigma_i^2 + \sum_i \sum_{j \neq i} w_i w_j \sigma_i \sigma_j \rho_{ij},$$

where ρ_{ij} is the correlation coefficient between the returns on assets i and j. Alternatively the expression can be written as:

$$\sigma_p^2 = \sum_i \sum_j w_i w_j \sigma_i \sigma_j \rho_{ij}$$

where $\rho_{ij} = 1$ for $i=j$.

- Portfolio return volatility (standard deviation):

$$\sigma_p = \sqrt{\sigma_p^2}$$

For a **two asset** portfolio:

- Portfolio return: $E(R_p) = w_A E(R_A) + w_B E(R_B) = w_A E(R_A) + (1 - w_A) E(R_B)$.
- Portfolio variance: $\sigma_p^2 = w_A^2 \sigma_A^2 + w_B^2 \sigma_B^2 + 2 w_A w_B \sigma_A \sigma_B \rho_{AB}$

For a **three asset** portfolio:

- Portfolio return: $E(R_p) = w_A E(R_A) + w_B E(R_B) + w_C E(R_C)$
- Portfolio variance: $\sigma_p^2 = w_A^2 \sigma_A^2 + w_B^2 \sigma_B^2 + w_C^2 \sigma_C^2 + 2 w_A w_B \sigma_A \sigma_B \rho_{AB} + 2 w_A w_C \sigma_A \sigma_C \rho_{AC} + 2 w_B w_C \sigma_B \sigma_C \rho_{BC}$

Step 1: Find the historical prices of the two stocks.

In order to do this, we need to find the stock symbol for Coca-Cola. We can do that by using Google and searching for "Coca-Cola stock". According to Google, the symbol is KO and it is traded on NYSE (New York Stock Exchange). Next, we will go to Finance.yahoo.com to find the historical prices. The next step is to search for "KO", the symbol for Coca-Cola that we found earlier and then click on "Historical Prices" (you can find this on the left side on the website). The last step is to get the **daily** prices. I decided to get the prices of the stock from the last 365 days. You can choose longer period of time, however it is not recommended to go over 5 years.

Do the same for Microsoft as-well. Go on Google, find that the symbol is "MSFT" and downloaded the **daily** prices for the last 365 days.

Step 2: Calculate standard deviation, correlation and set an expected rate of return

After downloading the historical prices of Coca-Cola and Microsoft, it is time to use them to create a portfolio. As it says above, it is time to calculate the standard deviation, correlation and set an expected rate of return. First of all, after downloading, you can see that there are 7 different columns in the Excel file: Date, Open, High, Low, Close, Volume and Adjusted Close. All you need is the closing price, so feel free to delete all the other columns. You need to put the historical closing prices of both companies into one spreadsheet. This is how it should look like:

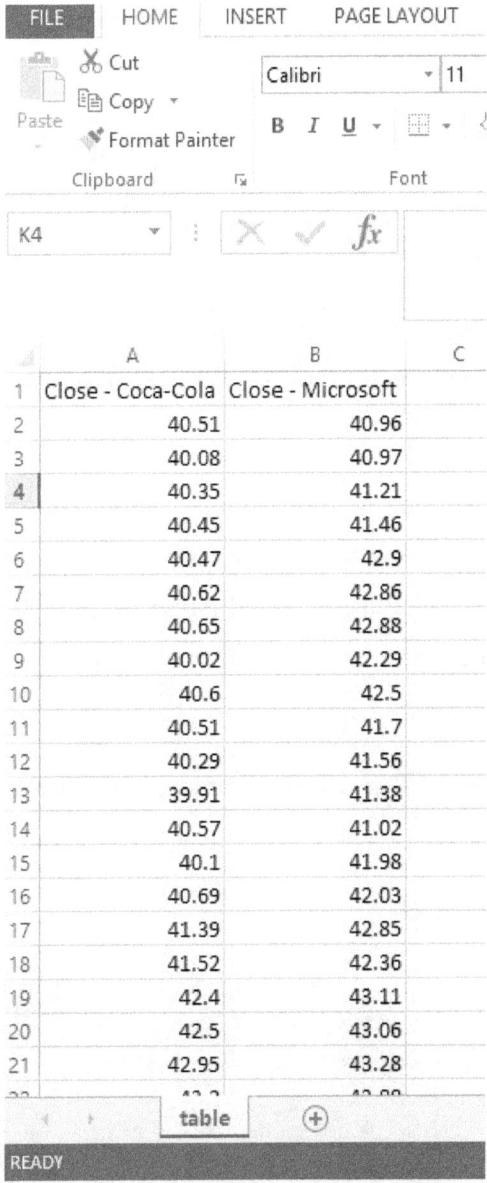

Now, we can calculate the standard deviation. Excel has an amazing formula for this purpose. The prices of Coca-Cola start at A2 and go all the way down to A252. We can calculate the standard deviation of the price of Coca-Cola by writing "**=stdev.s(A2,A252)**"

The prices of Microsoft start at B2 and go all the way down to B252. So, do the same for Microsoft, "**=stdev.s**(B2,B252)"

Now we have the standard deviation of the prices of both companies. Next step is to calculate correlation. The formula that we need is the following: "**=correl(A2:A252,B2:B252)**" This shows the correlation between the prices written from A2 to A252 and from B2 to 252.

** The correlation can range from -1 (perfectly negative) up to 1 (perfectly positive).

The last part of this step is to set an expected return. As you saw earlier, analysts have totally different opinions about the movement of the stock price. You can calculate the expected return based on historical data and check how much the price increased every year or you can use the median that the analysts predict.

I am going to use 18.1% as expected return for Microsoft and 10.2% as expected return for Coca-cola as that's the analysts' mean.

This is what I have so far.

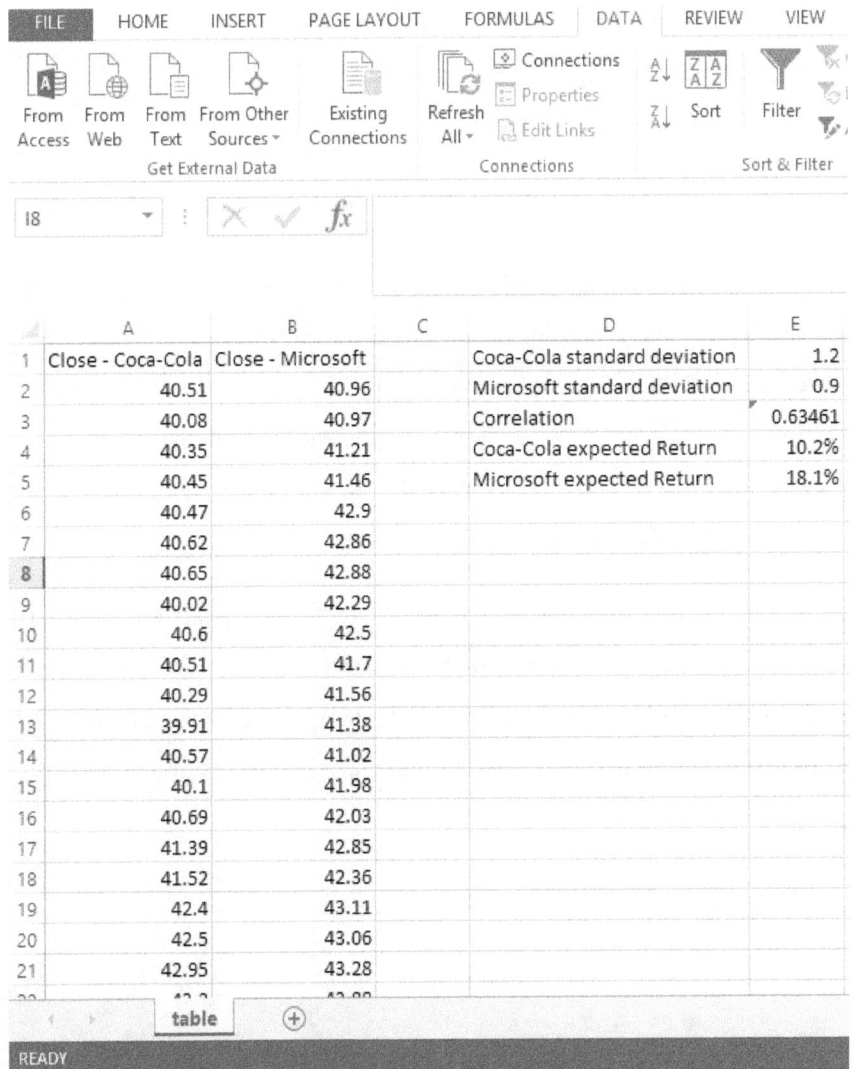

	A	B	C	D	E
1	Close - Coca-Cola	Close - Microsoft		Coca-Cola standard deviation	1.2
2	40.51	40.96		Microsoft standard deviation	0.9
3	40.08	40.97		Correlation	0.63461
4	40.35	41.21		Coca-Cola expected Return	10.2%
5	40.45	41.46		Microsoft expected Return	18.1%
6	40.47	42.9			
7	40.62	42.86			
8	40.65	42.88			
9	40.02	42.29			
10	40.6	42.5			
11	40.51	41.7			
12	40.29	41.56			
13	39.91	41.38			
14	40.57	41.02			
15	40.1	41.98			
16	40.69	42.03			
17	41.39	42.85			
18	41.52	42.36			
19	42.4	43.11			
20	42.5	43.06			
21	42.95	43.28			

** If you get different numbers it is okay. The prices that I used are not the same as the prices that you use.

Step 3: Add all of the information into one formula

Now you have all the information required for creating portfolio. It is a simple one and it only consists two different stocks, but it is a great example to understand how all of this works.

- Portfolio return: $E(R_p) = w_A\, E(R_A) + w_B\, E(R_B) = w_A\, E(R_A) + (1 - w_A)\, E(R_B).$

The participation of each stock as part of the portfolio is very important, in fact that's how we are going to optimize the portfolio. G2 will show the participation of KO's stock as part of the portfolio. I am going to write 50% for now. H3 will be 1-G2 and that means the rest of the portfolio will contain stocks of Microsoft. It is okay if you don't understand this yet, stick with me till the end and you will understand how it works.

According to this, the expected return is 50% multiplied by 18.1% (the expected return of Microsoft) plus 50% multiplied by 10.2% (the expected return of Coca-Cola). This is what I2 will show is, the expected return. I am going to calculate it as "=G2*E4+H2*E5".

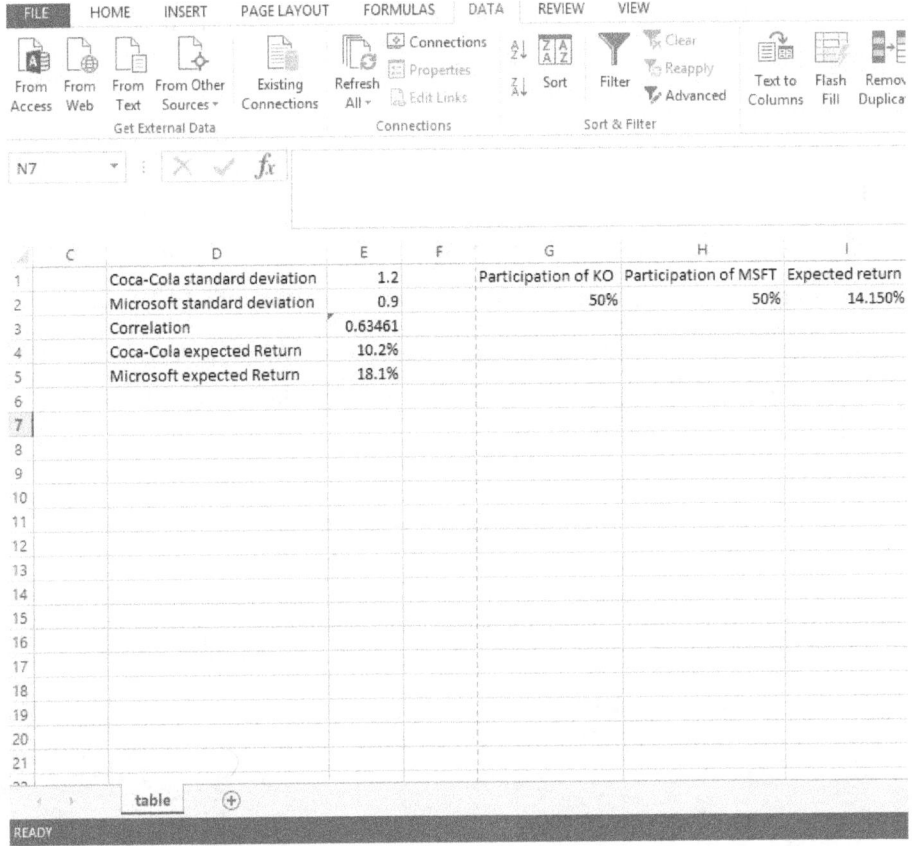

C	D	E	F	G	H	I
1	Coca-Cola standard deviation	1.2		Participation of KO	Participation of MSFT	Expected return
2	Microsoft standard deviation	0.9		50%	50%	14.150%
3	Correlation	0.63461				
4	Coca-Cola expected Return	10.2%				
5	Microsoft expected Return	18.1%				

As you can see, the expected return of the portfolio of 50% stocks of Coca-Cola and the rest 50% stocks of Microsoft is 14.15%. But, we mentioned in the first chapter that we are not only interested in the return, but also the risk. In order to add the last column that we need, we have to add one more formula.

- Portfolio variance: $\sigma_p^2 = w_A^2 \sigma_A^2 + w_B^2 \sigma_B^2 + 2 w_A w_B \sigma_A \sigma_B \rho_{AB}$

In my case, this formula in Excel would look like this:

"=(G2^2)*(E1^2)+(H2^2)*(E2^2)+2*(G2*H2*E1*E2*E3)" In this formula you can see which part of the formula means participation, standard deviation and correlation.

The last column that we need to create before we optimize the portfolio are related to this one. What I calculated now is not the standard deviation of the portfolio, but the variance. In order to calculate the standard deviation, I need to square root the variance. The square root formula in excel is "=sqrt(J2)". This is how everything that I just explained looks like in Excel:

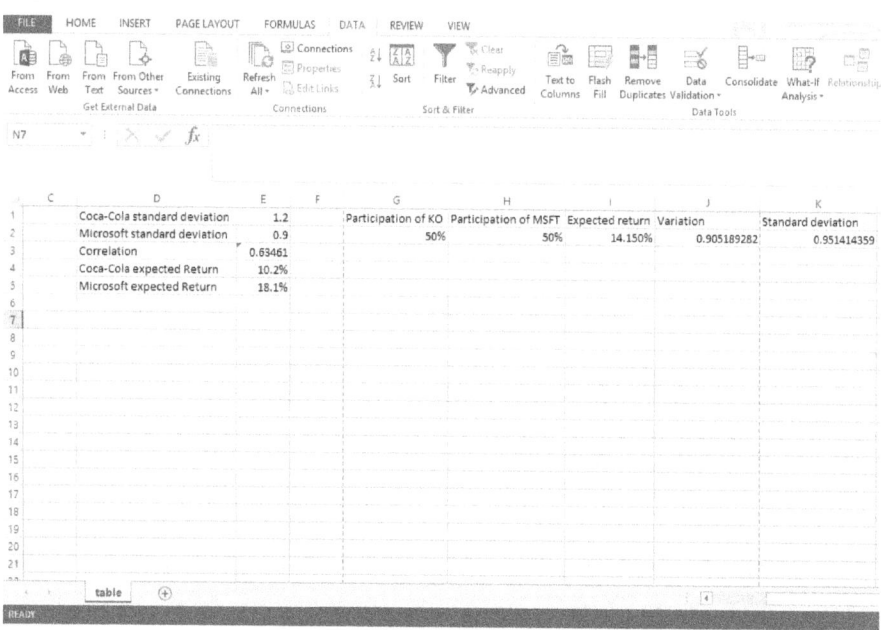

As you can see, the standard deviation of the portfolio is between the standard deviation of both stocks, but it is not the average. It is lower.

Step 4: Optimizing portfolio using Problem Solver

As we mentioned earlier, the standard deviation represents the risk. There is an amazing tool in Excel called Problem Solver (You can find it in Excel Options → Add-ins). This tool allows you to optimize your portfolio.

This is what the solver looks like:

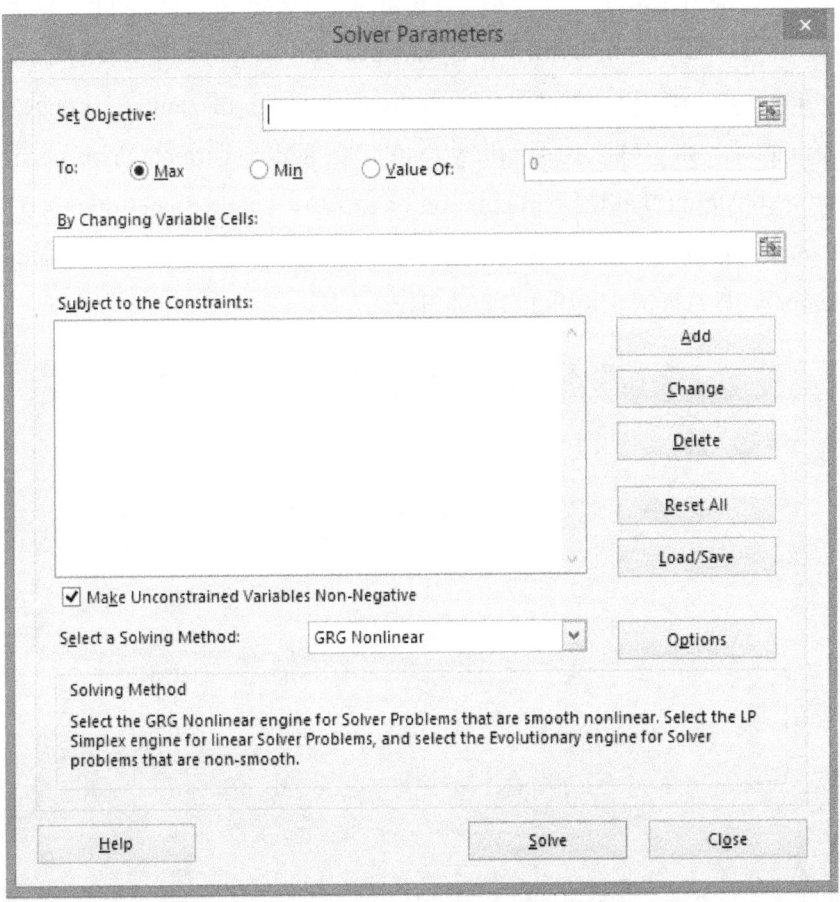

Now, as you can see, there is an objective you can set at the top. It could be either maximize the return by selecting Max or setting a value of desired return.

Example: Return of 14%

** The desired return has to be between the minimum and the maximum expected return by the individual stocks. It does not make sense to ask for a return of 25% in this case.

Select the Expected return of portfolio cell and set a value off 14%. Next, select the participation of KO as changeable variable cell. You don't have to add the participation of MSFT as changeable variable cell when you are optimizing portfolio of two stocks as the formula in this cell is 1 minus the participation of KO. Last of all, you need to add constraints. You need to add a constraint that the participation of KO is equal or higher than 0. This is important as Excel can come up with a solution that involves negative numbers. This is how it should look like:

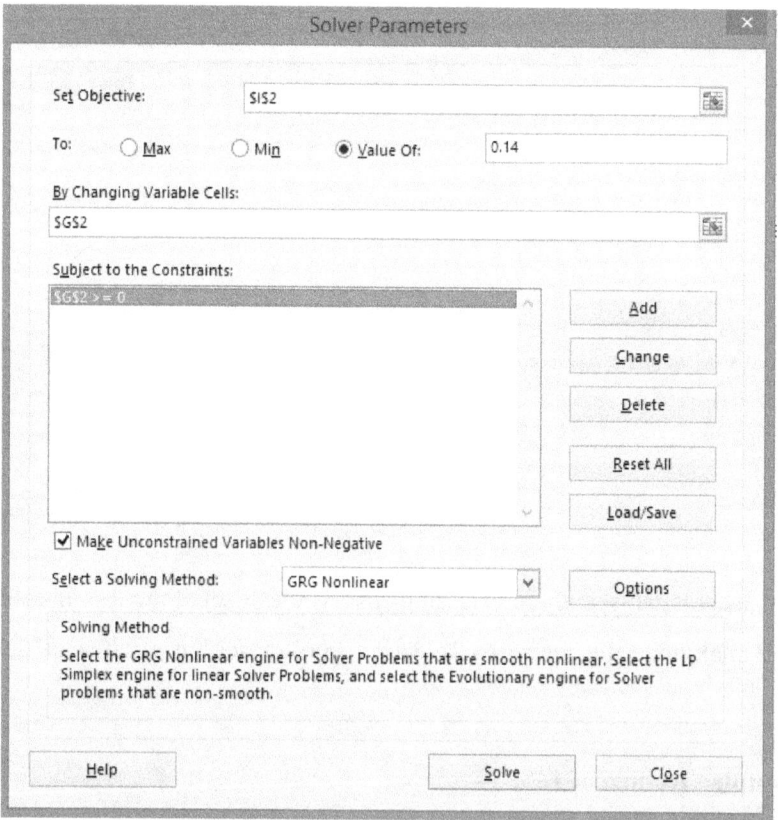

Once you click solve, Excel will find an optimal solution for your problem. In my case, it shows that I need a portfolio that consists 52% of Coca-Cola stocks and 48% of Microsoft stocks in order to get a return of 14%.

The second option that you have with Problem solver is minimizing the risk. This is the most important part in Portfolio optimization. Instead of maximizing or setting a value of the desired return, I am going to minimize the standard deviation of the portfolio. The changeable cells and the constraints stay the same.

But take a look at what I got as a result when I clicked solve:

D	E	F	G	H	I	J	K
Coca-Cola standard deviation	1.2		Participation of KO	Participation of MSFT	Expected return	Variation	Standard deviation
Microsoft standard deviation	0.9		14%	86%	16.980%	0.792336505	0.890132858
Correlation	0.63461						
Coca-Cola expected Return	10.2%						
Microsoft expected Return	18.1%						

What Excel is saying is that I get minimum risk if I create a portfolio that consists 14% stocks of Coca-Cola and 86% stocks of Microsoft. The expected return of this portfolio is 16.98%. But what is most important is the standard deviation. The standard deviation is **0.89**! Below the standard deviation of Microsoft. This is why portfolio optimization is important.

The example shows you the power of diversification. However, diversification with only 2 stocks is not enough. You can choose 3 or 4 or even more stocks that you think are good and then go step by step through the whole process. However, don't forget that if something happened in the past does not mean it will happen in the future as-well. So don't expect the exact same rate of return as that is what you expect. You'll often be wrong. However, what standard deviation means is it tells you how wrong you can be. But it does not mean that the return rate will be less. It only means that you will be wrong. You can also get higher return rate than the expected as-well.

Conclusion

Investing is not that simple as there are a lot of different strategies and software that might help you to come up with the best decision. However, none of that guarantees success. The only thing that is quite sure today are the Treasury bills, but not many investors choose to invest in them for the long-run as they offer very low interest rate. If you decide to invest, you can start with low sum of money and try different strategies. After a year or two, you can check which strategy suits you the best.

In this short book, you learn many valuable lessons about investing.

You learnt why investing is important and what compounding interest is. You learnt the relation between risk and return. You learn about value investing, diversification and most important of all, portfolio optimization in Excel.

I am going to post what the NYU professor, Damodaran, said about investing one more time.

"You can be right in your assessment of value and go bankrupt being right. Your friend can pick stocks based on astrological signs and make millions. Don't expect justice."

Author Bio

Manuel Taylor was born in a small town in south Macedonia. He spent the first 18 years of his life in his hometown. After finishing high school, he moved to the capital city and studied Accounting & Auditing for the next 4 years.

After finishing college, he went back in his hometown and spent the next 3 years working in one of the best companies there as an accountant.

He met his wife and now they have 2 children.

Manuel left the company and started working with students where he was teaching the basics of economics, finance, and accounting. He also spent a lot of time working as freelancer on different projects in his city.

Manuel is a respected accountant and a person with expertise in this area. Apart from teaching, he is writing business plans.

Today, he has his own consulting company with 6 employees.

Check out some of the other JD-Biz Publishing books

Gardening Series on Amazon

Country Life Books

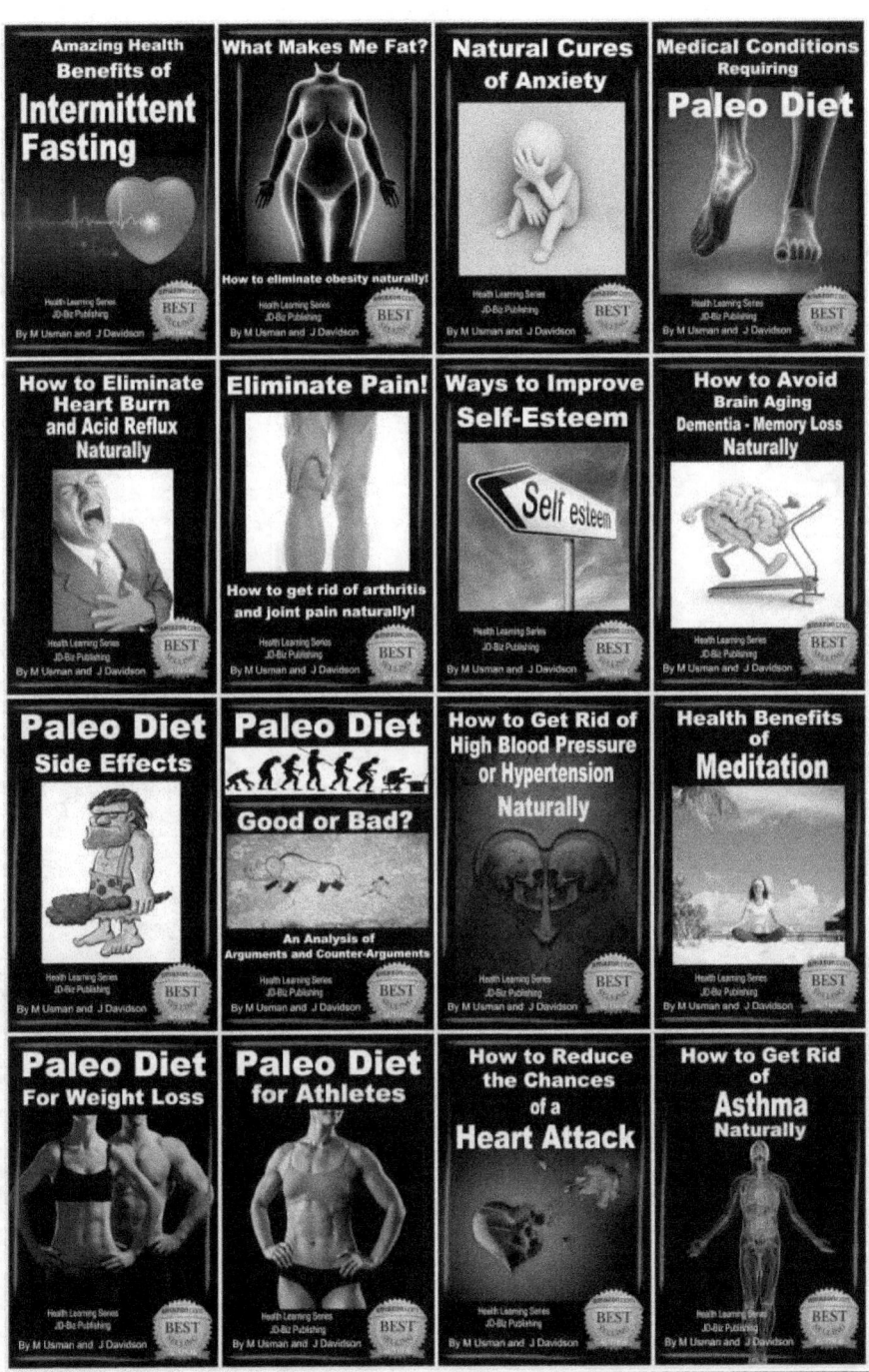

Amazing Animal Book Series

Learn To Draw Series

How to Build and Plan Books

Entrepreneur Book Series

Our books are available at

1. Amazon.com

2. Barnes and Noble

3. Itunes

4. Kobo

5. Smashwords

6. Google Play Books

Publisher

JD-Biz Corp

P O Box 374

Mendon, Utah 84325

http://www.jd-biz.com/

Mendon Cottage Books

P O Box 374, Mendon Utah 84325

Mendon Cottage Books